CAMBRIDGE LIBRARY COLLECTION

Books of enduring scholarly value

Cambridge

The city of Cambridge received its royal charter in 1201, having already been home to Britons, Romans and Anglo-Saxons for many centuries. Cambridge University was founded soon afterwards and celebrated its octocentenary in 2009. This series explores the history and influence of Cambridge as a centre of science, learning, and discovery, its contributions to national and global politics and culture, and its inevitable controversies and scandals.

Trinity College, Cambridge

Trinity College was founded in 1546 by Henry VIII, who merged two older institutions, Michaelhouse and the King's Hall. The beauty of Trinity's courts attracts visitors from around the world, but the College is also a thriving, modern community. This history, published in 1906, covers the period from the foundation until the early Victorian era, and will appeal to those interested in the history of both the college and the University. It is divided into chronological chapters, each illustrated by the series editor, Edward H. New. As Rouse Ball states, '... Trinity College Cambridge is the largest collegiate foundation at either of the ancient universities, and, few, if any visitors to Cambridge leave without walking through its courts. This booklet is written in the belief that there are many such visitors who would like to know rather more about the College than can be learnt from a stroll round its buildings.'

T0382301

Cambridge University Press has long been a pioneer in the reissuing of out-of-print titles from its own backlist, producing digital reprints of books that are still sought after by scholars and students but could not be reprinted economically using traditional technology. The Cambridge Library Collection extends this activity to a wider range of books which are still of importance to researchers and professionals, either for the source material they contain, or as landmarks in the history of their academic discipline.

Drawing from the world-renowned collections in the Cambridge University Library, and guided by the advice of experts in each subject area, Cambridge University Press is using state-of-the-art scanning machines in its own Printing House to capture the content of each book selected for inclusion. The files are processed to give a consistently clear, crisp image, and the books finished to the high quality standard for which the Press is recognised around the world. The latest print-on-demand technology ensures that the books will remain available indefinitely, and that orders for single or multiple copies can quickly be supplied.

The Cambridge Library Collection will bring back to life books of enduring scholarly value (including out-of-copyright works originally issued by other publishers) across a wide range of disciplines in the humanities and social sciences and in science and technology.

Trinity College, Cambridge

W.W. ROUSE BALL

CAMBRIDGE UNIVERSITY PRESS

Cambridge, New York, Melbourne, Madrid, Cape Town, Singapore,
São Paolo, Delhi, Dubai, Tokyo

Published in the United States of America by Cambridge University Press, New York

www.cambridge.org
Information on this title: www.cambridge.org/9781108017930

© in this compilation Cambridge University Press 2010

This edition first published 1906
This digitally printed version 2010

ISBN 978-1-108-01793-0 Paperback

This book reproduces the text of the original edition. The content and language reflect
the beliefs, practices and terminology of their time, and have not been updated.

Cambridge University Press wishes to make clear that the book, unless originally published
by Cambridge, is not being republished by, in association or collaboration with, or
with the endorsement or approval of, the original publisher or its successors in title.

The College

Monographs

THE COLLEGE
MONOGRAPHS
Edited and Illustrated by
EDMUND H. NEW

TRINITY COLLEGE,
CAMBRIDGE
W. W. ROUSE BALL.

ST. JOHN'S COLLEGE,
·CAMBRIDGE
THE SENIOR BURSAR.

KING'S COLLEGE,
CAMBRIDGE
C. R. FAY.

MAGDALEN COLLEGE,
OXFORD
THE PRESIDENT.

NEW COLLEGE,
OXFORD
A. O. PRICKARD.

MERTON COLLEGE,
OXFORD
REV. H. J. WHITE.

Fountain & King Edward's Gate

TRINITY COLLEGE

CAMBRIDGE

BY

W. W. ROUSE BALL

FELLOW OF THE COLLEGE

ILLUSTRATED BY

EDMUND H. NEW

1906: LONDON: J. M. DENT & CO.
NEW YORK: E. P. DUTTON & CO.

All Rights Reserved

PREFACE

SEVERAL years ago the Editor of the *College Monographs* conceived the idea of a series of volumes dealing separately with the Colleges of our two ancient Universities; since then many historical and illustrated works carrying out, in some degree, this idea have been published.

But the Editor believes that there is still a need for a set of short, well-written, and illustrated handbooks of moderate price.

The *College Monographs*, of which this volume is the first, have been planned to supply this need. They are written by members of the society with which they are concerned, and aim at giving (1) a concise description of the buildings, (2) a recital of the origin and history of the community, (3) an account of collegiate life, manners, and customs, both past and present, and (4) a record of distinguished sons; while each volume will contain

PREFACE

about fifteen illustrations of the most beautiful and characteristic buildings, as well as a plan showing the periods to which they belong.

It is confidently hoped that the series will prove attractive to members of the University, and to all who are interested in the several groups of College buildings, whether for their own sake or on account of their many and varied associations.

LONDON, *March* 1906.

CONTENTS

CHAPTER I

THE COURTS AND BUILDINGS

CONTENTS

CHAPTER II

SOME INTERIORS

CHAPTER III

KING'S HALL AND MICHAEL-HOUSE, 1316–1546

CHAPTER IV

FOUNDATION AND GROWTH OF TRINITY COLLEGE, 1546–1615

CONTENTS

CHAPTER V

THE COLLEGE FROM 1615 TO 1820

CONTENTS

CHAPTER VI

THE NINETEENTH CENTURY RENAISSANCE

LIST OF ILLUSTRATIONS

The Great Gate
TRINITY COLLEGE

Trinity College

CHAPTER I

THE COURTS AND BUILDINGS

THE royal and ancient foundation of Trinity College—as it is termed in the University bidding prayer—is the largest collegiate foundation at either of the ancient English Universities, and few, if any, visitors to Cambridge leave without walking through its Courts. This booklet is written in the belief that there are many such visitors who would like to know rather more about the College than can be learnt from a stroll round its buildings. It is hoped also that some of its members will be interested in possessing an outline of its history, and an account of the life of their predecessors in former times. In this and the next chapter, I describe briefly the buildings and walks, and in subsequent chapters I give a sketch of the history of the Society.

I may commence by reminding a reader who is a stranger to the place that the College is the home of a large Society, and, though its Courts are generally open to any

A

one, the interiors of its public buildings can be visited only at times when they are not being used by its members ; the hours at which they are open may be learnt by inquiry at the Porter's Lodge. For this reason I will describe first those parts which are generally accessible, leaving to another chapter the description of the interiors which are accessible only at stated hours.

Probably a stranger visiting the town will approach the College by Trinity Street from the direction of King's Parade. At the north end of this street is situated a striking cluster of buildings. On the west side, stands the Great Gate of Trinity ; close to this, is the College Chapel ; and immediately beyond that, the graceful brick front of St. John's College. Facing these, and on the east side of the street, are the Whewell's Courts of Trinity College, bordering an irregular green on which stands a lofty cross, marking the site of a church which some forty years ago was moved to Jesus Lane. Beyond this green are the Divinity Schools.

Trinity College was founded by Henry VIII. in 1546, and his statue occupies the niche on the street side of the Great Gate. Beneath his figure are seven panels. The central panel is occupied by a stone shield, bearing the arms of Edward III., namely, France ancient and England quarterly, with supporters. Below it is a tiny shield on which are painted the arms of Blythe, in whose wardenship the gate was begun.

The other six panels bear respectively the arms of Edward's sons with their names and titles. His second son, William, died in infancy, and therefore was given a shield argent blank ; the other sons bore their father's arms with labels of cadency. Below the central panel runs a scroll with the legend *Edvardvs Tertivs fvndator Avle Regis*, MCCCXXXVII. This Plantagenet reference requires a few words of explanation.

When Henry VIII. determined to establish a new College at Cambridge, the greater part of the area of the present Great Court of Trinity was occupied by two Colleges known as King's Hall and Michael-House, and traversed by a public lane. He closed the lane, compelled the two Societies to surrender to him their charters and buildings, and acquired the other property on the site. He then founded Trinity College, endowing it with the buildings and revenues of the two Societies whose corporate life had been extinguished, and adding considerable revenues taken from religious houses recently dissolved. It is believed that the academic life of the students, at any rate of King's Hall, was not interrupted during these proceedings, and that in fact it runs back without a break to the days of Edward II. Hence, although Trinity College dates from 1546, its history is inseparable from that of the medieval foundations on which it was erected.

3

The present Great Gate of Trinity had been constructed as the chief entrance to King's Hall, and completed in its present form only a few years before that Society was dissolved. The east side fronts the street. The west side, facing the Court, contains statues of James I., his wife, and his son Charles, commemorating the two royal visits to the College in 1615. We will suppose that the visitor enters the College by the Great Gate, and accompany him as he walks round the Courts.

Passing through the Great Gate a visitor will find himself in the Great Court of the College. This Court, as it now stands, is a quadrangle enclosing rather more than two acres. The general style of the buildings, save at the south-west corner, is late Perpendicular. On the north side are situated the Chapel and the Old Library ; on the west side are placed the Lodge, Dining Hall, Kitchens, and Combination Rooms ; the south and east sides are occupied by living rooms.

The present appearance of the Court differs widely from that at the time of the foundation of the College. The buildings of King's Hall and Michael-House were well adapted to the separate Colleges, but for a single Society they were not convenient in themselves or well placed relatively to one another. Their rearrangement gave some trouble to the new foundation. The parts of

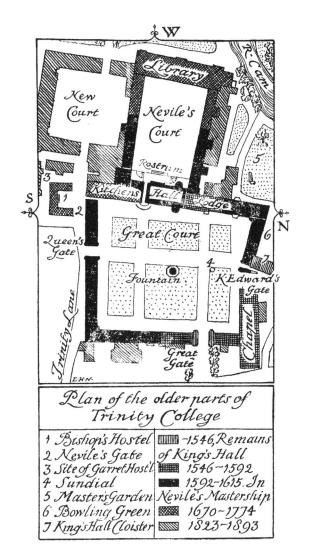

Plan of the older parts of
Trinity College

1 Bishop's Hostel	▥ −1546, Remains of King's Hall
2 Nevile's Gate	
3 Site of Garret Host'l	▦ 1546−1592
4 Sundial	■ 1592−1615. In Nevile's Mastership
5 Master's Garden	
6 Bowling Green	▨ 1670−1774
7 King's Hall Cloister	▧ 1823−1893

Michael-House which protruded into the present Court seem to have been pulled down at once, but a range of rooms of King's Hall, which extended from the east side of the Court about half-way across it, and another range, which ran from the west side up to the sun-dial and then northwards to the present Clock Tower, were left standing for a considerable time. Towards the end of the sixteenth century the College took in hand the reconstruction of its buildings; the projections into the Court were pulled down, and the Court arranged substantially as we now see it. The architect to whom the general plan was due was Ralph Symons, and perhaps this is one of the most successful of his efforts.

Turning to the right and walking round the Court, we come, between the Great Gate and the Chapel, to a staircase leading to various living rooms occupied by resident members of the College. We may take these as typical of the usual arrangements. The entry from the Court is unclosed by any door, and opens freely to the air. From it a staircase leads to the upper floors. On the entry and landings open solid doors known as "oaks," each leading to a set of rooms, and when the oak is shut or "sported" the rooms are isolated. Usually inside the oak is a second door opening on a sitting or "keeping" room, through which access is obtained to a bedroom and a

7

"gyp-room." Stores of all kinds are kept in the gyp-room, which derives its name from γύψ, a vulture. This bird was supposed to indicate the characteristics of the man-servant who looked after the rooms, but the gyps of to-day do not deserve such a re-proach. In recent buildings the oak often opens into a small lobby round which the rooms are placed, but this is a comparatively modern development. Of course the set occupied by a resident Fellow is more ex-tensive, and generally comprises at least two sitting-rooms, and often a spare bedroom. In former times water required for the rooms was drawn from some source elsewhere, and there was not a pipe or drain of any kind on the staircase. I believe that this contri-buted to the general immunity from epidemic diseases of those occupying College rooms.

Near the middle of the Court is the Fountain, a beautiful specimen of late Re-naissance work, erected in 1602, and rebuilt on the same lines in 1716. It is supplied with water by a conduit passing under the river. Originally, 1325, this conduit belonged to a Franciscan monastery which stood in Sid-ney Street; it was tapped by King's Hall in 1439, and granted to Trinity by Henry VIII. The College has the curious right of being able at any time to expose the conduit pipe for the purpose of executing repairs or alterations, and any one who builds or plants on land over the pipe does so subject to this easement. Its position across fields and roads in the country is marked by occasional small white posts marked T. C. P. Until comparatively recently it was from this fountain that the bedmakers, or College servants, in this Court drew the water required for domestic purposes.

This particular staircase, which I have taken as a typical one, contains one Fellow's set, five undergraduates' sets, one of which is now used by the porters, and an odd room. The rooms on the ground floor on the right hand side on entering the staircase were occupied by Thackeray, and later by the present Astronomer-Royal; those on the opposite side by Macaulay; the rooms on the first floor next the gate were occupied by Isaac Newton, and later by Lightfoot, afterwards Bishop of Durham, and R. C. Jebb, the Greek scholar; and those on the opposite side by J. G. Frazer, who has done so much to investigate the habits of thought of primitive man. This, is an interesting group of men, but in fact there are few rooms in the College which have not been inhabited at some time by those who have made their names famous. Since 1825 the College rent-books specify the names of the tenants; before then it is only by luck that we are able to identify the rooms occupied by particular people.

Proceeding round the Court we come next to the Chapel, commenced by Queen Mary, and finished in 1567 by Elizabeth.

It is 205 feet long and 33 feet wide. Originally the outside was covered with stucco,
but some thirty years ago the side next the
Court was faced with stone, and at the
same time a porch was added. On the
east end next the street is the inscription,
DOMVS MEA DOMVS ORATIONIS VOCABITVR.
This is a curious phrase to have used, since
those who placed it there must have had in
their minds the verse in Luke xix., which,
in the authorised version, runs :—" My
house is a house of prayer," and is followed
by the clause, " but *ye* have made it a den
of thieves." Wags have sometimes continued the inscription by adding the second
clause on the Chapel either of Trinity or
of St. John's as their inclinations led them.
The interior of the Chapel is described in
the next chapter.

Next to the Chapel is King Edward's
Gate, or the Clock Tower. It was erected
about 1427, where the sun-dial now stands,
and led to the main Court of King's Hall.
It had been so long connected with the
history of the College that, when the
Great Court was reconstructed, the gate
was preserved, taken down stone by stone,
and rebuilt in its present position.

Passing under this Tower we come to
the remains of the Cloister Court of King's
Hall, sometimes known as King's Hostel.
Much of this was pulled down in 1694,
but one side was left, though until recently
it was concealed by common brick facings.

These were removed in 1905, and the remnants of the old building repaired as carefully as possible. The front, which is a specially interesting piece of architecture some 500 years old, faces the bowling-green. The undergraduates' common room and the chapel vestries are situated here.

Returning into the Court and continuing our walk round it, we come next to a block which occupies the remainder of the north side of the Court. The doorway in it immediately next King Edward's Tower leads to the old bowling-green of the College, which runs behind this block and terminates in a terrace - walk along the river side. This was the pleasure-ground of King's Hall, and is an interesting old-world garden, but the public are not admitted to it unless accompanied by a Fellow. The upper storey of this block was built for a Library, but was turned into College rooms towards the end of the seventeenth century, when the new Library in Nevile's Court was completed. This range is finished by a corner turret staircase.

We come next to the west side of the Court. The long building between the Hall and the corner turret is the Lodge, where the Master of the College lives. Inside there is a valuable collection of portraits belonging to the College : the great staircase, state drawing-room, and dining-room are also well worth a visit, but these are not open to the inspection of strangers. The beautiful oriel window which formerly faced the Court was destroyed some 150 years ago.

The present oriel was erected in 1843 in accordance with a suggestion made by Beresford Hope. Congratulating Whewell on his election to the mastership, Hope expressed a wish to see the oriel replaced, and offered £300 for the purpose, adding that he was prepared to subscribe more if necessary. Whewell submitted the matter to the Fellows, who approved the plans, apparently in the belief that the work was a present to the College. The cost, however, far exceeded the first estimate. Hope paid £1000, Whewell £250, and the College had to find the remainder. While the Society was still sore from this unexpected demand, the Master, without consulting them, placed on the oriel the following inscription, which may still be read there : *Munificentia · fultus · Alex. J. B. Hope · Generosi · hisce · aedibus · antiquam . speciem · restituit · W. Whewell · Mag. Collegii.* A.D., MDCCCXLIII. The Fellows, who found themselves heavily taxed to meet the cost of what they regarded as a luxury, resented the omission of all mention of their own enforced contribution, and gossip—very likely unjustly—attributed to the influence of his wife the refusal of Whewell to contribute more.

I should hardly have mentioned this small squabble were it not for the following parody on *The House that Jack Built,*

which Tom Taylor (Fellow, 1841) wrote
on the occasion :—

" This is the house that Hope built.

This is the master so rude and so gruff,
Who lived in the house that Hope built.

This is the maid so tory and tough,
Who married the master so rude and so gruff,
And lived in the house that Hope built.

This is the inscription or rather the puff,
Placed by the master so rude and so gruff,
Who married the maid so tory and tough,
And lived in the house that Hope built.

These are the seniors who cut up so rough,
When they saw the inscription or rather the puff,
Placed by the master so rude and so gruff,
Who married the maid so tory and tough,
And lived in the house that Hope built.

This is the architect who is rather a muff,
Who bamboozled those seniors that cut up so rough,
When they saw the inscription or rather the puff,
Placed by the master so rude and so gruff,
Who married the maid so tory and tough,
And lived in the house that Hope built."

Next to the Lodge comes the Hall, erected
on the site of the kitchens of Michael-
House. The dimensions are almost exactly the same as those of the Hall of the
Middle Temple in London. It is entered
from a passage, approached by a semi-
circular flight of steps projecting into the
Court. Its interior is described in the next
chapter.

Adjoining the Hall is a range containing
the Combination Rooms on the first floor,

13

and the Kitchens on the ground floor. These apartments also are described below. This block, with its ugly classical façade, was erected about 1770, replacing a singularly graceful building of the late Renaissance. It is on the site of the dining-hall and other public buildings of Michael-House.

The south side of the Court is occupied by living rooms. It is pierced near the middle by the Queen's Gate, erected in 1597 to balance King Edward's Tower on the opposite side. The statue in the niche is of Queen Elizabeth, and below it are the arms of the College (namely, argent, a chevron between three roses gules, on a chief of the last a lion passant gardant between two books or). The shields on either side bear the arms of Nevile and Whitgift. The rooms between the Kitchens and the Queen's Gate are on the site of part of Michael-House.

The turret staircase at the extreme east end of this southern range, where it meets the east side of the Court, used to be known as Mutton-Hole Corner, a name which is believed to have been derived from the fact that a passage was made in 1655 from rooms on this staircase to the shop of the College chandler in Trinity Lane, and that, as candles were commonly made from mutton fat, the vicinity of the tallow vats gave rise to this name. It was on this staircase that Porson and Byron occupied rooms.

The east side of the Court between Mutton-Hole Corner and the Great Gate is also occupied by living rooms. The passage through staircase I. in this block leads to Lecture-rooms.

On the west side of the Court, between the Hall and the Kitchens, we noticed a flight of stone steps. They lead through a swing door to a passage—known as the Screens — where various College notices are put up. On the right of this passage are doors opening into the Hall, and on the left are the entrances to the Combination Rooms, Kitchens, Butteries, and Plate Rooms. Leaving any further mention of these interiors for the present, we proceed out of the Screens through another swing door at the end and emerge into Nevile's Court.

This Court is named after Thomas Nevile, Master of the College from 1593 to 1615, who, at his own expense, built the two staircases on each side which are nearest the Hall. Originally the building was in florid Elizabethan style, but in the middle of the eighteenth century it was altered on classical lines, though traces of the former decoration can be seen behind the pilasters.

The Court is sometimes used as an open-air lounge after concerts or parties in the summer—the openings towards the river and the New Court being closed with tapestries, the cloisters lit by electric light, carpeted, decorated with palms, and furnished with seats, &c. Shortly after the marriage of the

15

present King, who was and is a member of
the House, the College had the honour of
entertaining him and his bride at a ball
given in this Court. For this the central
space was roofed in with a tent and used
for dancing—the rooms round the Court
being employed for sitting out, &c. It is
said to have made a singularly effective room
for the purpose.

Facing us, as we come out through the
Screens, is the College Library. It was designed by Sir Christopher Wren, and erected
by the College towards the close of the seventeenth century, on the initiative of Barrow,
who was then Master. The frontage to the
Court is well worth study. The effect from
the Court is of a building in two storeys, the
lower part in Doric style, and the upper
in Ionic. In reality, however, the floor of
the apartment rests about half-way up the
Doric half. The wall-space above it is
occupied by book-shelves, and the room
is lighted by windows above them. This
ingenious construction enabled Wren to
give a beautifully proportioned apartment
without interfering with the architectural
effect of a building in two storeys. The
interior of the Library is described in the
next chapter.

The Court, as designed by Nevile, was
closed on the west side by a low wall, through
which a gate led into the open country.
The Library was built beyond this wall, and
the sides of the Court were prolonged so as

to complete the quadrangle. The terrace on which the Screens open is termed the Rostrum, and was designed by Wren to give a sense of unity to the Court.

Turning to our right along the Rostrum and descending the steps at the end, we pass along the north side of the cloisters. This walk is interesting in the history of science, inasmuch as it was here that Newton made his experiments on the velocity of sound in various media. Behind this cloister are annexes to the Library, and in particular a reading-room and reference library. The entrance to the main Library is at the end of this walk.

The cloister under the Library is open to the river as well as to the Court, the windows and doors on the river side being filled with open wrought-iron work of the seventeenth century. A stranger should pass through the door at the end of the north cloister on to the green bordering the river. In front of him are the paddocks of Trinity, terminated to the north by a chestnut grove. To his right are situated the buildings of St. John's College. To the left the Trinity Bridge, beyond which stretch, as far as the eye can follow, the "Backs." The river frontage of the Library should also be inspected.

Returning to the cloister under the Library and walking along it, we notice the view of the Backs through the iron screens. At all times this is a charming sight, but it is seen at its best on a moonlit summer night. At the end of this walk we come to the south cloisters along that side of the Court. On the staircase next to the Library, Prince Edward, the elder brother of the present Prince of Wales, lived in rooms No. 5 during his residence in College. The rooms below on the first floor (D. 3) were for many years occupied by Sir William Harcourt. Next to this staircase is an arcade leading into the New Court, and beyond this other staircases containing living rooms.

Passing through the arcade we come to the New or King's Court, erected by the College in 1823–25, and accommodating about 100 men. The internal arrangements are excellent, but the pseudo-Gothic style in which it is built is not happy, and is rendered the less effective by the use of stucco, though fortunately much of this is covered by creepers. On the east and west sides are towers. Among former occupants of rooms in this Court I may mention the names of Arthur H. Hallam and Arthur J. Balfour. The former, to whose memory Tennyson's *In Memoriam* was dedicated, occupied the rooms No. 3 on staircase G. from 1828 to 1832 ; the latter occupied the rooms No. 4 on staircase A. from 1867 to 1870.

The tower on the west side of the New Court faces an avenue leading to the Backs. This avenue is now more than 200 years old, and in spite of the utmost care it is to be feared that the trees cannot be preserved much longer. It is desirable to walk down it for the sake of the view. A few steps bring us to a stone bridge, built in 1763-65, crossing the river, which here is very narrow : the bridge is noticeable from the fact that it is constructed with cycloidal arches. The view from it is fine, particularly in the direction of St. John's. Beyond the bridge, on either side of the avenue, are paddocks used for hockey, lawn-tennis, &c. At the end of the avenue are some handsome wrought-iron gates. Beyond these and across the road are the Fellows' gardens : these are not open to the public. It may be mentioned that again a short distance beyond them is the older cricket and football field of the College ; while the lawn-tennis ground, and a second and larger cricket and football ground are situated somewhat farther to the south.

Returning down the avenue the visitor will notice on his right, after crossing the bridge, some low buildings where the brewery of the College was situated in days when the College brewed for itself. Immediately below them is a stage whence boats can be hired.

Passing through the New Court and out under the tower on the east side we come to the Bishop's Hostel, occupied by men's rooms. This building was erected in 1670-71 from a donation of £1200 given by Bishop Hackett of Lichfield, a former Fellow of the College—hence the name.

It is on the site of two medieval hostels known by the names of Ovyng and Garret.

In 1874 it was proposed to pull down the Hostel, and build a new Court on the site,

BISHOP'S HOSTEL

but finally it was agreed to repair it and put an L-shaped range round it. Passing the Hostel on our right we can go into Trinity Lane through Nevile's Gate, or, passing through a narrow passage on our left hand, we come out into the Great Court at its south-west corner.

Nevile's Gate is a good piece of early Jacobean work, and a lover of heraldry will find the coats of arms on it an interesting study. On the street front it is surmounted by the arms of James I., with supporters, flanked on either side by the badges of England and Scotland, a rose and thistle. In the spandrels of the arch are, on the one side, the arms of Nevile modern, and on the other, the arms of Nevile ancient, while on the piers are Nevile's arms as Master of Trinity and Master of Magdalene—namely, Trinity and Magdalene impaling Nevile. The appearance of the last-mentioned coat is explained by the fact that Nevile had held the mastership of Magdalene for a few years before coming to Trinity. The historic connection between the Neviles and Magdalene College is preserved to the present day, the gift of that College being now in the gift of the Nevile family. On the west front of the gate are the arms of Nevile with his family quarterings, and on each side is one of the two well-known Nevile crests. In the spandrels of the arch are, on the one side, the arms of Trinity College, and on the other, the arms of Thompson (impaling Selwyn) in whose mastership the gate was moved to its present position. On the piers are Nevile's arms as Dean of Canterbury and Dean of Peterborough—namely, Canterbury and Peterborough impaling Nevile. The gate originally stood in the wall which closed

Nevile's Court towards the west. It was moved about 1680 to the end of the avenue. In 1733 it was moved to a position in Trinity Lane some 80 feet south of where it now stands and made an entrance to the Fellows' stables. It 1876 it was moved to its present position.

There is yet one more block of College buildings which requires mention. This is the Court built by Whewell, 1859-67, and known by his name. It is divided into two parts, and runs from Trinity Street to Sidney Street. The chief entrance faces the Great Gate. It accommodates about 100 men. There are some interesting features in the architecture of the buildings, though the constricted space on which Whewell erected them, and his effort to get as many rooms as possible on a narrow area, render them less attractive than would otherwise have been the case. Their separation from the older part of the College has also been a disadvantage, but the College has recently acquired from the Town a right to make a subway connecting this Court with the Great Court.

The
Trinity Hall
College

CHAPTER II

THUS far I have described the general external appearance of the College to any one who walked through its Courts and walks, and I refrained from interrupting my narrative by describing the interiors of the various buildings we passed. I devote this chapter to giving a short account of the interior aspects of the Chapel, Hall, Combination Rooms, Kitchens, and Library.

When walking round the Great Court we passed on its north side the porch leading into the Chapel. Entering by this, we find the interior divided in two unequal parts, the east end being fitted up for worship, the west end forming an Ante-Chapel into which the door from the Great Court leads. The two portions are divided by a screen on the top of which is built the organ. The present building, which is on the site of the Chapel of King's Hall, was finished about 1567, and it is believed that the fittings with which it was then furnished were taken from the Chapel of King's Hall. The present stalls, panel-work, baldachino, and organ-screen were inserted at the beginning of the eighteenth century ; there is a tradition that the old stalls were then moved to St. Michael's Church in Trinity Street.

The Chapel is of poor design, and in 1870 it was proposed to rebuild it. It has, however, some architectural interest from having been built by the sister queens, Mary and Elizabeth, and this argument, combined with the fact that it was hallowed by the memories of many generations who had worshipped there, determined the authorities to preserve it. It was, however, felt that its condition was not worthy of the College, and a complete scheme of redecoration— suggested by Westcott and Lightfoot—was undertaken.

Passing under the organ-screen we enter the Chapel. The carved wood work is worthy of notice, particularly the scrolls round the arms placed above the panels. The Adoration of the Magi is delineated on the south wall, but with that exception the frescoes on the walls, advancing from west to east, represent Jewish heroes and teachers, leading up to John the Baptist and the Mother of Christ on the east wall. Below the figures are trees, or plants, which are, or may allegorically be, associated with their careers or teaching. The design on the roof illustrates the " Benedicite," the words being painted as a frieze ; and, advancing from west to east, it is designed to lead up to the " Manifestation of God " indicated at the east end. There are fifteen windows, each containing eight

26

figures.   Taking them from east to west
they represent men prominent in the history
of Christianity and learning, especially as
related to the College.

According to this scheme, if we proceed
eastwards we are supposed to note in order
the frescoes on the walls and painting on the
roof, leading up through Jewish history to
the birth of Christ, and then, returning
westward, to have suggested to us, by the
successive windows, the historical development of Christianity, and the growth of
learning particularly in the University and
College.   It is certain that a man might
worship many years in the Chapel before he
discovered the symbolic meaning of these
decorations.

At the east end the visitor will do well
to examine the baldachino, which, though
heavy, is finely carved.   The panels in the
sacrarium are replaced by intarsia work in
which all the woods used are of their
natural colours.   The sixteenth - century
silver cross on the Communion Table
came from Spain.   The wrought - iron
work of the gas standards here and through
the Chapel are also worthy of note ; fortunately they were allowed to remain when
the electric light was introduced.   It may
be added that Bentley, the famous scholar,
is buried on the north side of the Communion Table.

Returning westwards we face the organ.
This, which replaced the old organ of King's

Hall, was built by Smith at the close of the seventeenth century, but it has been reconstructed more than once, and very little of the original work remains. It is a fine instrument, but too powerful for the building in which it is placed, and its immense size is out of all proportion to its location.

At Cambridge all undergraduates, bachelors, and members of the foundation wear surplices on Sundays and certain other days, in this differing from the usual Oxford rule. The effect when the Chapel is filled with a congregation all of whom, save for a few visitors in the stalls, are robed in white, is very impressive.

Returning to the Ante-Chapel, attention should be paid to the statues of Newton, Bacon, Barrow, Macaulay, and Whewell. All of them are good, notably those of Newton and Bacon. That of Newton is by Roubiliac ; it bears the inscription *Newton qui genus humanum ingenio superavit*, and perhaps it was only of Newton that such a remark could be truthfully made. It is said to be a faithful presentation of him in later life. The tombs of Porson, Dobree, and Whewell are among those in the Ante-Chapel. The windows here are not specially worthy of notice. The vestry and choir-rooms open out of this building, and from them access may be obtained to King's Hall Cloister Court.

Another group of buildings with which the daily life of members of the College is intimately associated is that containing the Hall, Combination Rooms, and Kitchens. All of these may be entered from the Screens.

Entering the Hall by the swing doors at its south end we find ourselves in a lofty apartment about 100 feet long, 40 feet wide, and 50 feet high. Facing us, as we enter, is the main body of the Hall, in which are placed five broad tables running lengthwise. The tables and benches are some centuries old. At the farther end is a raised dais occupied by two tables placed crosswise at which the Fellows dine. By the side of the dais and at the end of the main body of the Hall are two oriel windows, projecting respectively into the Great Court and Nevile's Court, and fitted with serving tables, &c. The Hall will accommodate comfortably some 250 men at dinner, about 150 at examinations, and about 600 or 700 at lectures, concerts, &c. The building is used for lectures in the morning and dinner at night. Lunch is also served here at midday, but attendance is optional.

Until forty or fifty years ago the building was warmed only by means of a great brazier which stood immediately below the lantern, the latter being unglazed and left open so as to allow the fumes of the charcoal to escape. This was a common arrangement until after the eighteenth century, and the discomforts must have been considerable. To those sitting near the brazier the heat was almost intolerable, but the parts distant from it were

29

hardly warmed at all, while the fumes of the charcoal and the draughts were everywhere perceptible.

The Hall is panelled. The carved wood-work of the screen over the entrance, and of the panels on the dais is noticeable ; all this is of the same date as the Hall, 1604–8. The wood-work on either side of the Hall is comparatively modern, as dry rot had got into the old panelling there.

Hung in the Hall are some interesting portraits, which in most cases are described by labels attached to their frames. In particular the visitor will like to look at the portraits of Maurice and Clerk Maxwell on the east wall ; of Tennyson (by Watts) and the Duke of Gloucester (by Reynolds) on the east wall of the dais ; of Newton, Bacon, and Barrow, as also a fine copy of Moro's portrait of Queen Mary on the end wall ; of Thompson (by Herkomer) and Thackeray on the west wall of the dais ; of Lightfoot and Benson in the west oriel; and of Vaughan (by Ouless) and Whewell on the west wall. Among the canvases above the panelling are portraits of the Earl of Macclesfield, 1666–1732; John Wilkins, Bishop of Chester, 1614–1672 ; Pearson, the divine, 1613–1686; Cowley, the poet, 1618–1667; Richard Bentley, the scholar, 1662–1742 ; Robert Smith, the mathematician, 1689–1768 ; Dryden, the poet, 1631–1701 ; and Coke, the Lord Chief Justice, 1549–1634.

The armorial bearings in the windows

are also well worthy of attention. From
time to time the College has accepted
shields of its benefactors or distinguished
sons. But the matter has never been taken
up systematically; and many arms that we
should expect to find are absent. The arms
of the present King and his eldest son are in
the west oriel. Another interesting pane in
this oriel is the outlined figure of Richard
Duke of York and Earl of Cambridge, the
father of Richard III. This is believed to
have been moved here from King's Hall;
it is one of the earliest portraits on glass
now extant in England. The arms bla-
zoned below are later than the figure.

Over the Screens at the south end of the
Hall is a Minstrels' Gallery, concealed by
carved wood-work, but open to the Hall
when the panels are removed. This gallery
is used by the choir on certain occasions,
when they sing glees after dinner. From
it, is obtained an excellent view of the Hall.

Returning from the Hall to the Screens,
we find on the opposite side of the passage
a staircase which leads to the Combination
Rooms and the Minstrels' Gallery. The
Combination Rooms are the private apartments of the Fellows.

The larger Combination Room is used
for wine after dinner, and for meetings of
all kinds during the day. It is sometimes
used also as an overflow dining-room if more
accommodation is wanted than is provided
in Hall. Some of the pictures in it are

good. In particular the visitor may like to look at those of the Duke of Somerset, 1662–1748, the "proud Duke," Chancellor of the University for sixty years; of the Marquess of Granby, of fighting fame, by Reynolds; of Isaac Newton in early life; and of Lord Halifax, his friend and patron, by Kneller. Of other portraits in the room, that of the Duke of Gloucester, 1776–1834, is by Opie; that of the Duke of Sussex, 1773–1843, is by Lonsdale; and those of the Marquess of Camden, 1759–1840, and the Duke of Grafton, 1760–1844, are by Lawrence.

The smaller Combination Room is used as a reading and writing room during the day, and as a smoking and card room after dinner. The walls are covered with engravings of former members of the College.

Below the large Combination Room are the Kitchen Offices. The Kitchens themselves, which date from 1605, can be entered either by a passage from the Screens or directly from the Great Court by a door in the middle of the block containing the Combination Rooms. The introduction of modern methods of cooking has robbed the Kitchen of many picturesque adjuncts, but with its high-pitched open roof and ancient fireplace it is worth a visit. The Plate Rooms and beer-cellars can also be seen.

The Library may be inspected by visitors, not accompanied by a Fellow, for an hour in the afternoon on days when it is open. It is some 200 feet long, rather more than 40 feet wide, and rather less than that high, and from the swing doors at the north end a general view of the interior is obtained. The book-shelves are ranged against the walls with projections into the apartment dividing it into thirty recesses. To conceive the Library as Wren designed it, we must suppose the dwarf bookcases down the centre and in the various recesses to be removed, and each recess to be occupied either with some work of art, or with a table and stools for the use of students. Some of these tables and stools, made under his directions, are still *in situ*. Four of the recesses are closed by carved doors for the safer custody of works of value, and the attendants are not allowed to show these to visitors.

The ends of the bookcases projecting into the room are ornamented with carvings by Grinling Gibbons. It was originally intended to place statues on the tops of the cases, and pedestals were provided, but the present arrangement by which these are occupied by busts seems preferable. On the floor and close to these cases are stands supporting marble busts of distinguished members of the College. The pavement is laid in black and white marble.

The Library is a storehouse of literary and artistic treasures of inestimable value. A visitor interested in such matters might

easily spend weeks or months examining
what has been here collected. Among objects
which are not kept in the locked recesses he
will, even if pressed for time, like to look
at the selection of illuminated manuscripts
placed on the dwarf bookcases at the south
end of the Library. Close by is Milton's
manuscript of his *Minor Poems*, and his first
sketch of *Paradise Lost*, which he com-

CARVING IN LIBRARY BY GRINLING GIBBONS

menced in the form of a drama. In other
cases here are the fifteenth-century manuscript account of the battle of Agincourt
set to music, the original manuscripts of
Thackeray's *Esmond*, and Tennyson's *In
Memoriam*, the copy of Lord Bacon's *Opera*
with his holograph inscription offering it to
the College, and a selection of some of the
rarest and earliest printed books.

At this end of the Library also is a marble

statue of Lord Byron by Thorwaldsen. It had been intended for Westminster Abbey, but as it was refused by two successive Deans who objected to the poet's opinions, it was offered to his old College, where it finds a fitting home.

CHAPTER III

KING'S HALL AND MICHAEL-HOUSE
1316–1546

THUS far I have been concerned chiefly with the buildings of the College. We must now turn to the history of the Society that occupies them. The following pages are summarised from a sketch on the subject which I wrote for my pupils in 1899.

I have already stated that the history of Trinity College is closely connected with that of King's Hall and Michael-House. It will be convenient to preface what I have to say about those ancient foundations by a few words on the medieval University of which they formed a part.

The University of Cambridge originated about the end of the twelfth century. At first the students lived in lodgings, but, by the close of the medieval period, we find all, or nearly all, of them living in Monastic Hostels, Colleges, or Private Hostels. Of these the Colleges alone survived the Renaissance. The Monastic Hostels were maintained by religious orders for the reception of those of their members who were studying at the University. These ceased

The
Library

to exist with the suppression of the mother houses at the Reformation. Private Hostels were for the reception of Pensioners, *i.e.* of students who paid their own expenses, which for an average student came then to from £9 to £14 a year. A private hostel was managed by a master of arts who lived in it; it resembled in some respects a boarding-house at a modern public school, and maintained a continuous life. At the close of the medieval period there were seventeen of these hostels recognised in the University. Many of them belonged to Colleges who had purchased them as investments, and let them at a rack-rental. In the early part of the sixteenth century the number of students at Cambridge decreased, and the stress produced thereby fell heavily on the non-incorporated hostels. When the numbers of the University began to increase again, the Colleges admitted Pensioners, and the Private Hostels ceased to exist.

The Colleges, of which before the Reformation there were fifteen, were usually founded to provide homes for students, and thereby free them from the temptation to join a religious order. Pensioners may have been occasionally admitted as a matter of favour, but practically membership was confined to those whom we should now term Fellows, Scholars, and Sizars. The members were generally under an obligation to say masses for the souls of their founder and his kin. The Colleges provided board, lodging, and pocket-money for their members, also, what was especially valued, the use of a Library. Except for Peterhouse, the two earliest Colleges were King's Hall and Michael-House ; they were also among the most important of these foundations.

King's Hall was founded by Edward II.

THE GREAT COURT

between 1307 and 1316. At first its members occupied hired houses, but in 1337 Edward III. established them in a building of their own on a site occupying the north-east plot of the present Great Court : this is believed to be the building known to Chaucer as Solar Hall. This was not the only benefaction conferred by Edward III., and the Society paid him no idle compliment when they described him as their founder, though their statutes show that they recognised that the title was technically due to Edward II. Solar Hall was built of wood, and in the last quarter of the fourteenth century the Society erected more substantial buildings. Originally there were only twelve scholars besides the Warden, but, within a few years of its foundation, the numbers had risen to about forty. It was an aristocratic foundation, and, almost alone among medieval Colleges, did not require poverty as a qualification for membership. According to its statutes of 1380, scholars were not admissible unless at least fourteen years of age, and sufficiently instructed in grammar to be able to study dialectics ; they were required always to speak Latin or French. The Society seems to have flourished, and in 1546, when dissolved, there were fifty resident members of the foundation, and the income exceeded £210 a year.

Michael-House was founded in 1324— also in the reign of Edward II.—by Stanton, a notable lawyer and statesman of the time. It was designed for the reception of a Master and six poor scholars, and the members were required to be priests, or at least in orders, within one year from their admission. Later benefactors increased the foundation by two Fellows, three Chaplains, and four Bible Clerks ; it always remained closely connected with the secular clergy. Towards the close of the fifteenth century it received numerous gifts, and, in 1546, when dissolved, the income exceeded £140 a year.

The details of the external history of King's Hall and Michael-House need not detain us further, but it may be well to give an outline of the daily life of their members. The students of the two houses can have had little in common. Michael-House was a small Society, with most or all of its members in orders, and (except perhaps the Bible Clerks) there can have been few of them under age : indeed here, as in most of the medieval Colleges, the number of those whom we should term Scholars was small compared with the number of those whom we should describe as Fellows. On the other hand, at King's Hall, there seems to have been a body of students corresponding to undergraduate scholars of to-day. It is to students of King's Hall that most of what follows is directly applicable.

Assuming that a lad commenced residence when about fourteen years old, his first three or four years of residence were devoted to Latin, logic, and selected parts of Aristotelian philosophy. During this period he was for most purposes regarded as a schoolboy, but at the same time he was treated as a member of the community and though subject to discipline he had recognised rights.

At the end of this time the student was

admitted to the title of bachelor, and the next four or three years were usually given up to logic, metaphysics, and philosophical questions connected with theology. The bachelors took part in the instruction of the younger students, and for disciplinary purposes occupied a position somewhat similar to that of undergraduates nowadays.

At the end of the seventh year from entry the student who had performed all necessary exercises could proceed to the degree of master. We may think of him as being by this time about twenty-one years of age. He was then obliged to teach for at least one year in the University. If he continued in residence he would probably proceed in due course to degrees in other faculties.

To qualify for a degree it was necessary to perform various exercises in the University, and especially to keep a number of *acts* or to oppose acts kept by other students. An *act* consisted in effect of a debate in Latin thrown, at any rate in later times, into syllogistic form. It was commenced by one student, the respondent, stating some proposition, often propounded in the form of a thesis, which was attacked by one or more opponents, the discussion being controlled by a graduate. At King's Hall (and in other Colleges) assistance was given in preparing for these trials, and in particular numerous private acts were kept, at which all the members were expected to be present, and in which they had at different times to take part.

Perhaps on a typical day a collegian, on rising, maybe about 5.0, attended early mass, though this does not appear to have been compulsory. This seems to have been followed by a light meal paid for by the students, and therefore taken only by those who could afford it. After this the student went to lectures until, say, 9.30—the lectures consisting generally either of dictation from text-books or of formal analyses of arguments and sentences. Occasionally, however, an enterprising lecturer would propound a proposition which, as the case might be, he defended or attacked against the arguments of his class. About 10.0 the student dined in Hall, and after that he was expected to work again for a couple of hours or more. If he escaped having to spend the afternoon in attending or keeping acts, he could use it as he willed. Supper was commonly served in the Hall about 5.0. From then to Compline his time was at his own disposal. Possibly light refreshments were obtainable before Compline, after which came bed. Meat was provided at dinner and supper except in Lent. The monotony of life was relieved by entrance feasts on the admission of a new member, funeral feasts in memory of the virtues of former benefactors, and various functions on saints' days and other special occasions. Most of the students resided through the Christmas and Easter vacations; the rigour of discipline was then somewhat relaxed, and it was not unusual to perform plays and give entertainments.

The amusements of the students were much what we should expect English lads to have indulged in. Contests with the cross-bow were common, and cock-fighting was not unusual. Fishing was popular, and perhaps not the less so because exercised in violation of the rights of the Town. To the more adventurous, the opportunity of a fight with other gownsmen or with townsmen was open, and often ended in bloodshed. Besides these recreations, tournaments and fairs were constantly held in the immediate neighbourhood, to the detriment of discipline, but to the pleasure of the younger students. Among the more wealthy members of the University, bull-baiting, tennis, and riding seem to have been specially favoured ; many Colleges had private open-air tennis-courts. Among other provisions of the statutes of King's Hall, I notice that students were not allowed to keep dogs in College, or to play the flute to the annoyance of their neighbours : the additional provision that no scholars should use bows or pea-shooters within the House must commend itself to every one of mature age. Chess and games with dice seem to have been familiar, though illicit, indoor pastimes. It should be noted that many of the above amusements were against the rules, but the fact that they were constantly forbidden is rather an indication that they were not unknown than that they were never enjoyed. Of the amusements of the older members we speak with less certainty. Probably some of the dons were mere recluses, but riding, hunting, hawking, and tennis were not unusual.

The students dressed much like other Englishmen of the period. Perhaps knee-breeches, a coat bound round the waist with a belt, stockings, and shoes fairly represent the visible part of the dress of an average student. To this attire most men added a cloak, edged or lined with fur, which often found its way into the University chest as a pledge for loans advanced. At King's Hall the younger students were required to wear a *robam talarem decentem et honestam pro statu clericali*, and the bachelors and graduates a *robam cum tabardo gradui suo competentem.* Masters and doctors wore a square cap or biretta. Probably until the sixteenth century junior students went bareheaded. The shape of the hoods for bachelors and masters has not changed since the thirteenth century.

Nevile's Court

CHAPTER IV

FOUNDATION AND GROWTH OF TRINITY
1546-1615

I LEAVE now the subject of life at King's Hall and Michael-House to turn to the history of the College which succeeded to their buildings. Two days after the surrender of their charters and property, Trinity College was founded by royal charter, December 19, 1546. At the same time Henry pensioned or dismissed the Master and most or all of the Fellows of Michael-House, whilst he appointed Redman, who had been Warden of King's Hall, Master of Trinity, thus definitely linking its life to that of the royal Edwardian foundation. The connection of Trinity with Michael-House is much less intimate. Henry endowed his new College liberally, adding to the belongings of King's Hall and Michael-House property, producing over £1400 a year.

The foundation of the College was contemporaneous with the introduction into the University of new studies and a new system of education, and the College was intended to be a centre for the propagation of the tenets of the reformed faith. Of the sixty original members whom Henry nominated, it is said that all were Protestants; many of these did not act on the nomination, but in 1548, apart from pensioners and fellow-commoners, there were 110 members of the foundation. Under statutes issued in 1552 the number of Fellows was fixed at fifty, of Scholars at sixty, while that of Pensioners was not to exceed fifty-four. It was further ordained that every student should be under a Tutor who was responsible for his instruction.

I think we may say that from its foundation the College has always recognised that it was its duty to be a centre of learning as well as a place of higher education. Thanks to its traditions and the large number of resident Fellows, the College has been able to take up this double duty.

The protestant character of the foundation was emphasised during the reign of Edward VI., and the Roman vestments, &c., used for service in King's Hall Chapel were sold in 1550. They realised over £140 and must have been very valuable. At the same time the altar and altar-steps were removed, and a communion table was set up, placed, as far as I can gather, near the middle of the Chapel.

Queen Mary took a warm interest in the College, perhaps through the influence of the then master, Christopherson, who was her chaplain and confessor. One of the earliest works undertaken under her impulse was the erection of a new Chapel, and of course the Roman service was restored. She further augmented the revenues of the Society by a gift of land producing £338 a year, and it continued to grow apace. In 1564 the number of residents was returned as 306, the total number of residents in the University at the time being 1267 : it is possible that servants are included in these returns, but at any rate about a quarter of the resident University were members of the College. At a slightly later date, 1573, the total number of residents at Trinity and of residents in the University were returned as 393 and 1813 respectively ; in 1641 they were returned as 277 and 2091 ; in 1672 as 400 and 2522 ; and in 1796 as 558 and 2137. Since 1796 the University calendars give the numbers each year. In the Michaelmas Term, 1905, the number of resident undergraduates, B.A.s, and higher graduates were respectively 568, 65, 135 in the College, and 2835, 363, and 642 in the University.

The statutes of 1552 and 1560 regulated the daily life of members of the House in minute detail. It would seem that an undergraduate was expected to rise at 4.30, and, after saying his private prayers, to attend Chapel service at 5.0. He then adjourned to Hall for breakfast, during which meal Scripture was to be read and expounded. From 6.0 to 9.0 the lessons learnt on the previous day had to be recited and those for the next day learnt—the subjects of study for undergraduates being Latin, mathematics, dialectics, and philosophy, and for bachelors philosophy, perspective, astronomy, and Greek. At 9.0 the students were expected to proceed to the public schools, either to hear lectures or attend public disputations. Dinner was served at 11.0, and at 1.0 the students returned to their attendance at the exercises in the schools. From 3.0 until 6.0 in the afternoon they were at liberty to pursue their amusements or their private studies; at 6.0 they supped in Hall, and immediately afterwards were supposed to retire to their chambers: there was no evening service on ordinary days until the reign of James I. Their seats in Chapel, their behaviour at home and abroad, their dress, their incoming and outgoing, and even their amusements were prescribed, and the punishments for breaches of rules defined. But it is doubtful whether this was more than a statement of what was deemed desirable.

The College grew and prospered during the reigns of Edward VI. and Mary, but it did not escape the troubles caused by the religious controversies of the time, though probably the old faith had no very large following within its walls.

In the reign of Elizabeth the rapid increase in numbers of a party that desired further changes on presbyterian lines, created a position of considerable difficulty. The leader of the puritan party in the College and University was Thomas Cartwright, who, though educated at Clare and St. John's, was elected to a fellowship at Trinity in 1562. During the next few years he and his friends are said to have organised and taken part in various unseemly attacks on those current opinions and ceremonies which they disliked—especially the administration of the Communion according to the authorised service-books. Their actions on these matters may well be buried in decent obscurity, but two examples of their conduct on more trivial questions may be quoted. One was a turbulent demonstration in the College Chapel on a Sunday evening, when they appeared without surplices. The other was their breaking those Chapel windows " whearin dyd appeare superstition." The conduct of the puritan leaders on such matters caused widespread distrust of their judgment and sense of responsibility.

The then master, Beaumont, fell largely under puritan influence, and in 1564 expressed his disapproval of students taking part in dramatic representation, and in the following year, with other Heads, protested (though without effect) against the order directing the use of the surplice in Chapel. He died in 1567, leaving a request to be buried with " no vain jangling of bells nor any other popish ceremonies." He was a weak leader to guide the College through such troubled times, and discipline became seriously relaxed under his rule.

It was only a strong and somewhat arbitrary man who could have put an end to the rising disorder. The man was found in Whitgift, subsequently Archbishop of Canterbury, who was made master of the College in 1567. He devised the measures which placed and retained the control of the University and Colleges in the hands of the anglican party, and the University statutes, which he suggested and which rendered this possible, remained in force until 1856. Thus we may say that his policy practically dominated the University for nearly three centuries.

At the time of his appointment to the mastership he was known as a man of strong character, but though attached to the State Church he belonged to the moderate party, and was sincerely anxious to avoid unnecessary strife—he had, for instance, signed a protest against the compulsory use of the surplice in Chapel. He was, however, determined to maintain order, and deeply resented the violence of the puritan leaders.

Cartwright at this time was denouncing the Church of England in his lectures and sermons, and in days when news-sheets were almost unknown and books comparatively rare, lectures and sermons materially influenced opinion. The scandal was so serious that the Chancellor wrote to the University on the subject : the reading of his letter was followed by a stormy scene which showed that matters had come to a crisis. Whitgift urged that it was necessary to strike at the root of the disorder, and that the statutes of the University should be revised. His advice was taken, and the result was the Elizabethan code of September 1570.

The importance of the new statutes lay in the fact that they revolutionised the machinery of government, and enabled the

THE COLLEGE ARMS ON QUEEN'S GATE

Heads of Houses to control all business. The new statutes, however, were also concerned with the order of studies and the maintenance of discipline. Hereafter an undergraduate was obliged to be a member of a College. In order to graduate he had to reside for three years and study classics, arithmetic, rhetoric, and logic ; he was then

55

created a "general sophister." Next he kept certain acts and exercises (*see* above, p. 43), and, if approved, was termed a "questionist." Finally he was examined by the proctors and any masters who wished, and, if approved by them, he proceeded in due course to the degree of bachelor. The regulations about the M.A. degree soon fell into disuse, and need not detain us here. These statutes mark the close of the period of transition, 1535 to 1570, between the medieval University and what we may call the collegiate University.

In the autumn of 1570, Whitgift was elected Vice-Chancellor. He at once expelled Cartwright from his professorship, and a few months later deprived him of his fellowship at Trinity on the ground that he had not taken priest's orders as required by the statutes. Another prominent puritan, Travers, left the College in order to avoid expulsion. "I was forced," wrote Whitgift, " by due punishment so to weary him, till he was fain to travel and depart from the College to Geneva, otherwise he should have been expelled for want of conformity towards thei orders of the house, and for his pertinancy."

Whitgift and his party were determined that their breach with the puritans should not excite any suspicion that they were leaning to popery. It was well known that Dr. Caius adhered to the old rites, and that he possessed a private collection of vestments and service-books. Under an order obtained from London, Whitgift ransacked the collection, and, "toiling resolutely and perspiring," he personally threw the "popish trumpery" into a bonfire lit in the Court of Caius for the occasion.

Whitgift had the interests of the College at heart, and where theological doctrines were not involved he took broad views. Two instances will suffice. When St. Peter's College, better known as Westminster School, was founded, an effort was made to associate it with Trinity College, Cambridge, and Christ Church, Oxford, on lines similar to those connecting Winchester and New College, or Eton and King's College. This would have been a misfortune for all concerned. Whitgift resolutely opposed the policy. As a compromise the College agreed to give seven scholarships every three years to nominees from the school : this was extended a few years later to cover the award of three scholarships every year. This question came up more than once in the subsequent history of the College, and was not finally settled till 1857. On a somewhat similar issue he tried, in 1576, to obtain an Act of Parliament to render illegal the sale of fellowships and scholarships ; this did not become law till 1589. After that, royal interference at fellowship and scholarship elections was not unknown, but though the College could not directly resist the orders of the Crown, an irregular custom of pre-electing to vacancies grew up which afforded means of evading the royal commands.

The numbers of the College did not increase under Whitgift's rule, nor was it desired that they should do so. It already numbered between a quarter and a fifth of the members of the University, and it has never been the policy of the College to increase indefinitely. But the class of students attracted was somewhat changed by the partisan character of his rule—many scholars withdrawing from a Society where liberty of thought was so strictly defined. He acted as Tutor, and in this work was successful ; among his pupils I may mention Essex, subsequently the ill-fated favourite of Elizabeth, Francis Bacon, and Edward Coke. One of his tutorial ledgers, showing the accounts sent to his pupils, is extant, and in my sketch of the History of the College I have printed extracts from it.

An interesting picture of Whitgift in his daily life is given by a contemporary. "The students," says Sir George Pawle—

"he held to their publique disputations, and exercises, and prayers which he never missed, chiefly for devotion, and withall to observe others' absence, alwaies severly punishing such omissions and negligences. He usually dined and supped in the common Hall, as well to have a watchfull eye over the schollers, and to keepe them in a mannerley and awfull obedience, as by his example, to teach them to be contented with a scholler-like College diet."

58

That he was a stern disciplinarian there can be no doubt, and in some regulations issued by him he directed that for certain offences undergraduates should be whipped publicly in Hall and in the schools, and that Bachelors should be kept in stocks in the College for a whole day as well as fined.

In 1577 Whitgift accepted a bishopric and resigned his mastership. A farewell sermon preached in the College Chapel from 2 Cor. ch. xiii. verse 11, revealed an unexpected affection for the place, as well as powers of oratory which moved his audience, "insomuch that there were scarce any drie eyes to be found amongst the whole number"; and so amid signs of genuine esteem he left for a wider sphere of action.

It is difficult to over-estimate the effect of his rule. He revolutionised the governing machinery of the University; he enormously increased the powers of the Master in every College; and he secured to the Church of England the control of the University. That he acted unselfishly for what he believed to be the good of the College is unquestionable. He was an excellent man of business. It is true that he was a harsh disciplinarian; but it may be doubted if gentler methods would at that time have been equally efficacious in maintaining discipline; and judged by almost any test we may say that, though he was unscrupulous and his actions often unconstitutional, yet the College prospered under his rule.

The year 1593 is memorable for the appointment to the mastership of Thomas

NEVILE'S GATE

Nevile.   Building on the site of the Great
Court had taken place at intervals since the

foundation of the College, and it had been recognised from the first that the site offered opportunities for the creation of a stately Court worthy of the reputation of the College ; but the progress made had been slight, and at the date of Nevile's appointment many of the buildings round the Great Court were still mean and in bad repair. He realised more fully than his predecessors how much the effect would depend on the magnitude of the site, and probably it was due to him that the north side of the Court was placed as it is, and not in a line from the Great Gate westwards as had been originally proposed. To obtain funds he got a license from the Crown authorising the College to grant long beneficial leases, and with the fines received for such leases and some private benefactions, he was able to begin operations. But though the Society supported Nevile, he was the author of the scheme, and without his assiduity, tact, and generosity, it could not have been brought to a successful issue.

On the " reconcination " of the Court I need add nothing to what I have said in the first chapter. Save for the Great Gate, the Chapel, and King Edward's Gate, the buildings are substantially due to Nevile. Its appearance has been but little altered since it was finished, except for the ugly kitchen block erected in 1770–5. The general effect was universally admired. Thus

Fletcher, writing about 1610, in dedicating a work to Nevile, said—

> " I think (King Henry the 8 being the Uniter, Edward the 3 the Founder, and yourself the Repairer of this College wherein I live) none will blame me, if I esteem the same, since your polishing of it, the fairest sight in Cambridge."

It is worth noting that Fletcher treats the life of the College as being continuous with that of King's Hall, and this I believe to be the correct view.

The Great Court is not the only memorial of Nevile's work, for, as I have already stated, he erected at his own expense, at a cost of some £3000, four staircases (two on each side) in the Court since known by his name.

The old tennis-court of the College had been destroyed in connection with the work on the east side of the Great Court, and a new one was now erected between Nevile's Court and the river at a cost of £120. The popularity of the game is shown by the fact that two keepers of the court, or markers, were permanently employed by the College. This court was destroyed when Wren built the present Library, and it was not then rebuilt.

The custom of the Judges of Assize staying in College during the sittings of their Courts in Cambridge arose through Nevile's hospitality. Among his friends was Coke, subsequently Lord Chief Justice, who, when a barrister, was always a welcome visitor at the Lodge, and the hospitality seems to have been continued when he became Chief Justice of the Common Pleas. After Coke's death the reception of the Judges was continued intermittently, but in 1662 the custom seems to have been recognised, and in 1866 was put on a legal footing.

Nevile's reconstruction of the College buildings was finished about 1612, and was made the occasion for asking Prince Charles, afterwards Charles I., to visit the College, 1613. Two years later, James I. came. Nevile was then dying, but by his directions the Court was entertained in the most sumptuous manner—to gratify his Majesty the "taking tobacco" in Hall being strictly forbidden. So pleased was the King that within two months he came for a second visit, but a few days before his arrival Nevile passed away, lamented by every member of the College which he had so faithfully served and loved. James paid other visits in 1623 and 1624, accompanied on the latter occasion by Prince Charles, whose betrothal to Henrietta of France was ratified while he was here, and Charles I. came again in 1632 and 1642.

I have alluded exclusively to the material benefits which Nevile conferred on the House, but it must not be inferred therefrom that he failed to maintain worthily its fame and repute. Indeed he was able to refer with just pride to the fact that at the same time the Lord Chancellor, the Lord Chief Justice, the two Archbishops, and numerous of the most eminent statesmen, lawyers, and ecclesiastics of the day were members of the foundation over which he presided.

His face is familiar from the portrait which the College has hung in the place of honour in the dining-room of the Lodge. He took no part in politics. On ecclesiastical questions he was a pronounced though moderate anglican, but he enjoyed the respect of all parties, and faithfully lived up to his well-known motto, *Ne vile velis*. Besides holding various honourable offices, he was successively Dean of Peterborough and of Canterbury : a memorial of his connection with the last-named city has been preserved in the magnificent Canterbury psalter which was obtained through him, and which is now one of the treasures of the Library. But it is his tact, hospitality, and boundless generosity which the College still gratefully remembers as the prominent features in his character : " he never had his like," said Hacket, " for a splendid, courteous, and bounteous gentleman."

By this time the manner of life in College had come to differ in many respects from that of medieval times. Externally, spacious courts and handsome buildings had replaced the small quadrangles and dingy hostels of the earlier period. But the internal changes were more important. In the first place only a small proportion of students, other than Fellows, continued to reside after graduation. This change removed a valuable link between the senior and junior members of the body. As far as the undergraduates were concerned, the extinction of the private hostels and the commingling of scholars and pensioners under one roof tended to the advantage of all. But the admission of large numbers of pensioners led to serious overcrowding, four or more undergraduates often sharing a single room, though the disadvantage was minimised by the construction in the larger apartments of cubicles. Pensioners formed the bulk of the residents, and at Trinity a considerable proportion of these were sons of squires or merchants. The cost of education of a pensioner seems to have been about £45 a year. Boys were still sometimes admitted, but sixteen was a not unusual age at which to commence residence.

The College appears to have been to a large extent a self-contained community with numerous servants. It had its own kitchen, buttery, bakery, brewery, barber's shop, and so on, and no one was allowed to deal outside the walls for anything thus supplied by the authority of the College. Besides these there were stables, storehouses, and numerous out-buildings which we see now only in some large isolated house or farm.

With the advent of the Renaissance there had been a marked change in the subjects of higher study. During the medieval period the prevalent subjects had been scholastic philosophy and theology, but at the close of the sixteenth century the subjects usually read by students comprised biblical criticism, classics, logic, mathematics, and ethics. The result of this change was far reaching.

The actual instruction was now mainly in the hands of College officials, and University exercises and lectures were with the exception of certain necessary "acts," neglected or treated as a formality. College instruction was given in classes, probably on somewhat the same lines as form-teaching in a public school to-day. The printing press encouraged the production of text-books, and their comparative cheapness rendered it possible for students to procure copies of their own. Hence men were able to study for themselves in a way which had been impossible in the Middle Ages. The tutorial system was similar to that now in force except that any Fellow could, subject to the approval of the Master, take pupils.

As to discipline, trivial breaches of rules were punished by fines or impositions. More serious breaches were punished, so far as *non adulti* were concerned, by corporal punishment, and the Dean attended in Hall to see that the birch was applied to such students, and sometimes also to any lad who was beginning to show himself "too forward, pragmatic, and conceited." Punishment of the older students seems to have consisted generally of fines, impositions, being placed out of commons, or being confined to the walls of the College, but occasionally an offender was carried ignominiously through the College on a "stang" or pole. Corporal punishment seems to have been always confined to those *non adulti*, and thus as the age of entry rose the use of the rod died out.

The civil and religious discussions of the day were keenly debated, and probably there were but few students who were not prepared at a moment's notice to explain and defend the most abstruse doctrines of politics and theology. The majority of the senior Fellows were moderate anglicans, but many of the younger Fellows and undergraduates preferred a presbyterian form of government.

The dress and amusements of students were much the same as those of other English lads of the same rank. At this time archery, tennis, and football seem to have been the most popular forms of exercise. The last-named game was a rough affair, and often followed by fights ; for this reason inter-collegiate matches were forbidden in 1579. The College played on the green between the College and the river. Sports and games, however, were

unorganised, and it was not until the first
quarter of the nineteenth century that their
conduct was undertaken by permanent clubs.
On the other hand, dinners and entertainments were constantly given, and much
hospitality shown in connection with them,
though already these were somewhat disliked by the more extreme precisians.

What, however, I desire chiefly to empha-
sise is that undergraduates then, like their
predecessors in medieval times, were in
essentials much the same as their successors
to-day. The fields were as green and the
sky as blue then as now. It is true that
customs were coarser, the hours of work,
meals, and play were different, and discipline
was harsher ; but these are the accidents of
life, and not essentials.

Nevile's Court and the Library

CHAPTER V

THE COLLEGE FROM 1615 TO 1820

THE period immediately succeeding Nevile's death does not seem to have been one of particular interest. The College prospered, and no marked changes in its policy or habits became prominent. Probably on the whole the presbyterian party gained strength in the College, especially among the junior members; but, though their leaders were sincere, clever, and energetic, they did not secure the confidence of their opponents. I think the cause is to be found partly in the intemperate hostility they showed to all who differed from their views, and partly to the irritation felt at their objections to the time-honoured and harmless hospitalities and small courtesies which tend, especially in collegiate society, to make the wheels of life run smoothly.

About this time the fall in the value of money caused a considerable increase in the revenue of the House, and at the same time rendered the statutable stipends inadequate for the maintenance of the Fellows. After some discussion it was decided, in 1630, to divide the surplus in certain proportions among members of the Society, and from this originates the current system of fellowship dividends.

During the early part of the seventeenth century, the College seems to have been especially favoured by the poets. In particular, I may mention George Herbert, Fellow from 1614 to 1628, Abraham Cowley, Scholar, 1637, and subsequently Fellow, and Andrew Marvel, another Scholar of this time, who graduated B.A. in 1638. Dryden entered a few years later.

The fact that the Master was appointed by the Crown, and that, by the statutes, he had large powers in determining the policy of the College, tended to keep the Society in general harmony with the views prevalent in London. At the same time it is easy to exaggerate the influence exerted by the Masters. On many matters they were content to accept the position as one of dignity and ease, and, unless their personal interests were touched, to let matters take their own course. This may explain why the appointment, in 1625, of Mawe, who was an extreme advocate of the views of Laud, seems to have exercised but little influence on the policy of the College. The numbers, however, at this time began to fall, and simultaneously the High Church party made some progress in the College. In 1635 they were sufficiently strong to secure the re-arrangement of the Chapel in accordance with their views—it being agreed to move the Communion Table from near the middle of the Chapel to "the upper end, and the ground to be raysed, and that the chappell be adorned accordingly."

The coming civil disturbances were already affecting the College. The number of residents fell rapidly, and in 1638–9 and 1639–40, the admissions sank to nineteen and eighteen respectively. In 1640 the superstitious found a presage of the coming troubles in the fact that for a short time the water of the Cam turned " red as blood." They had not long to wait for the fulfilment of the omen, for in little more than a year Cambridge began to feel the direct effect of the civil commotions, and in yet another year the disturbances were serious. In 1642 we read of muskets being fired into College windows, and the University ordering fifteen chestfuls of weapons to protect itself. The mayor tried to intercept these and secured ten, " but the scholars of Trinity College had just taken five of them before the mayor knew thereof." In June Cromwell seized the Castle, and in August assumed the command of the town, which remained under the control of Parliament for the rest of the war. In this year, 1642–3, the College admissions sank to thirteen, probably the lowest on record.

In 1643 Cambridge was close to the field of operations. The College was occupied by troops, and, in the scheme of fortification adopted, the Trinity and Garret

73

Hostel bridges were destroyed. In the same year the Chapel was " reformed " by Parliament ; but exactly what was done I do not know, save that "four cherubims and steps were levelled," the " figures " were whitened, and the organ hangings and rails removed. This was but a small matter, for in fact troops were quartered in the College, and practically its revenues sequestrated. The College petitioned the House of Lords on the subject, and, in June 1644, the Society was put under parliamentary protection.

In 1642 the bulk of the College plate had been sent to the King at his request, and it would seem that the residue was sent early in 1644. The immediate and natural effect of this gift was the ejection of the Master and Fellows responsible for it ; this was followed later by the removal of forty-two more Fellows : among the more distinguished of those expelled were Thorndyke and Babington, the divines, Cowley the poet, and Sir Thomas Sclater, a benefactor of the House. Throughout the subsequent Commonwealth period most of the fellowships were filled by Parliament or Cromwell, and rather as a reward for political zeal than for learning. The fact that the place was now free from warlike operations led to a considerable rise in the number of students.

The Heads successively appointed by Parliament were narrow partisans, and College life was carried on under the most

74

intolerant rules. I think that loyalty of members of a corporation never shines more brightly than in times of stress, and in this crisis some members of the College, notably Duport and Ray, devoted themselves to keep alive the traditions of scholarship. The same party, in 1659, petitioned for the appointment, as Master, of Wilkins, an Oxonian, one of the founders of the Royal Society, and a man of culture and learning. He had married the Protector's sister, and doubtless owed the preferment to this fact, for his sympathies were royalist and anglican.

There is an amusing account of a fellowship election just after Wilkins' appointment, which illustrates life under the zealots. During a game of tennis in the College Court, one of the scholars was struck in the eye by a ball, whereon Creighton, then a fellowship candidate, who was in the court, cried out, " O God, O God, the scholar's eye is stroke out." For this remark he was accused of profanity as one who took God's name in vain, and to confirm the accusation it was further added that he never came to the private prayer meetings in which the puritan students indulged. It was lucky for Creighton that Wilkins had succeeded to the mastership. He treated the charge as a trumpery affair, and added that it did not signify much if Creighton neglected to come to the prayer meetings, " since he never failed in public [worship] nor his tutor's lectures."

75

Wilkins was the author of some amusing books. One, on the possibility of a journey to the moon, provoked the Duchess of Newcastle to ask him where she could find a place to bait if she tried the journey. "Madam," said he, "of all the people in the world I least expected that question from you, who have built so many castles in the air that you may lie every night in one of your own."

Wilkins' relations with all members of the House, save a few fanatics, were happy, and general regret was felt when he left the College at the Restoration. His cession of the mastership was due to the fact that Charles I. had promised it to Ferne, one of his chaplains, as soon as there should be a vacancy. On the Restoration Ferne's claims were acknowledged and he was admitted.

Ferne was a man of sincere piety and lovable disposition, and the College was fortunate in the appointment. Of course the use of the anglican services was renewed, matters replaced as far as practicable on their former footing, and all ejected Fellows restored to their rights ; but Ferne persuaded the College to recognise also as Fellows all those nominated under the Commonwealth, only stipulating that they should not preach in Chapel unless they were members of the Church of England. Similar moderation was shown by the College in other matters.

The restoration of learning in the College was encouraged by the presence of Pearson, the eminent divine, and Barrow, whose fame as a preacher and mathematician still survives. The latter had a ready tongue. When applying in 1660 for Orders he was questioned by a pedantic chaplain. Here is the dialogue :—Chaplain : *Quid est fides ?* Barrow : *Quod non vides.* Chaplain : *Quid est spes ?* Barrow : *Magna res.* Chaplain : *Quid est caritas ?* Barrow, *Magna raritas.* On which the chaplain retired in dudgeon, and reported to the Bishop that there was a candidate for ordination who would give him nothing but "rhyming answers to moral questions." But the Bishop, who knew Barrow by repute, was content. Barrow's teaching will always be memorable from the fact that it was under him that Isaac Newton, who entered Trinity in 1661, studied mathematics.

Newton kept a diary from which we can form a fair idea of the course of education at the period, and it is a course of which the College has no reason to be ashamed. It included Sanderson's *Logic*, Euclid's *Geometry*, Oughtred's *Clavis* (chiefly arithmetic), Descartes' *Géométrie*, Kepler's *Optics*, Victa's works, Van Schooten's works, and Wallis' *Arithmetica Infinitorum*. No doubt this was the course selected by an exceptionally gifted student, but it proves that the College was worthily maintaining its traditions of learning.

Newton's manuscripts show that in 1665, the same year in which he took his B.A. degree, he discovered the binomial theorem and had already invented fluxions. His theory of gravitation, his optical researches, and other investigations followed at no very distant interval ; the *Principia*, however, was not finally published till 1687. He resided continuously in College till 1696, and by his influence and lectures created a mathematical school which has profoundly influenced the history of Cambridge.

The revolution of 1689 secured to the College its rights and privileges, which, during the previous forty years, had been frequently violated by external interference.

From this time forward we can describe life in College in considerable detail. At the end of the seventeenth century, morning chapel was at 6.0, or perhaps 5.30. Breakfast was often taken at a coffee-house, where the London news-sheets could be read. Morning lectures began at 7.0 or 8.0 and were given in Hall, different tables being set apart for different subjects, such as logic, ethics, classics, and mathematics. Dinner was served about noon. In the afternoon there were disputations in the schools on themes such as "The doctrine of the eternity of punishment is inconsistent with the doctrine of the omnipotence of the Deity," or "Newton's method of prime and ultimate ratios is correct." Evening chapel was at 5.0. Supper was served in

78

Hall, perhaps about 6.0. Some of the Tutors gave lectures in their rooms in the evening. Once a week there was an oral examination in Latin of all students. Amusements were becoming less rough. Bowls, tennis, riding, shooting, and hunting were as ever popular; we also begin to hear of dining clubs. The age of entry [1] had risen to about eighteen. To the dons the College offered a comfortable home until there was an opportunity for a College living, and it must be admitted that some were content to consider it as nothing more.

From 1700 to 1742 the mastership was occupied by Richard Bentley. His writings are justly reckoned among the glories of Cambridge scholarship, but as Master of the College his career was marked by malversations of a scandalous character. Action was taken against him. He was condemned by every Court before which he was brought, and ordered to be expelled from the mastership, but partly by unscrupulous diplomacy, partly by availing himself of legal technicalities, he constantly delayed the execution of the sentence. Finally, in 1734, he offered his opponents that if they would leave him the title and emoluments of his office he would no longer interfere in the govern-

---

[1] The average age at the commencement of residence of a student pursuing the normal course was 18.03 in 1700, 18.69 in 1750, 18.83 in 1800, 19.48 in 1850, and 18.97 in 1900.

79

ment of the College, or in appointments to offices, fellowships, or scholarships, all of which he had been inclined to treat as in his private gift and to be awarded as he pleased without regard to merit or character. He was then old and failing in health, and

THE BRIDGE

as an end to his mal-government could not be long delayed, the proposal was accepted.

During the residue of Bentley's mastership the form of constitutional rule was restored, and the arrears of business of all kinds which had accumulated during his neglect of his duties cleared off. It would seem that it was at about this time that the modern tutorial system was introduced under which only two or three Fellows are appointed to act as Tutors instead of permitting every Fellow, subject to the Master's approval, to act as such. It became usual for each Tutor to appoint an Assistant-Tutor as his colleague, and the two men provided all the lectures and instruction for all students under them ; this arrangement encouraged a system of private tuition or coaching, of which both the ablest and the least in-dustrious students freely availed themselves.

Throughout Bentley's rule the position and reputation of the College steadily de-clined. No doubt there were scholars— for instance, Cotes, the most brilliant of Newton's pupils, Robert Smith, the mathe-matician, and Colbatch and Middleton, the literary critics — but the energies of all residents were largely taken up in the endless efforts to procure protection from Bentley's acts. The average entry in the forty-two years, 1701–42, including migra-tions and exceptional admissions, was only 27.8 a year.

Of Bentley's scholarship it is difficult to speak too highly ; no one was better quali-fied to form an opinion on this than Porson. "When I was seventeen," said he, "I thought I knew everything ; as soon as I was twenty-four, and had read Bentley, I found I knew nothing." So also, according to Mr. Kidd, Porson once, in conversing with a North

Briton, sketched the prominent features of Bentley's literary character with an enthusiasm which so interested his acquaintance that, before they parted, he ventured to inquire if Bentley were not a Scotchman. As I yield to no one in my admiration for the Scotch, I may complete the story which Mr. Kidd leaves unfinished : "No, sir," said Porson, " he was a scholar."

But though we may well accept the opinion that Bentley was the foremost scholar and critic of his day, and may readily admit that on matters on which his personal interests were not concerned he desired to promote the interests of learning, no one can justify his conduct as Master. It is indisputable that he deliberately appropriated money and property belonging to the College, and that many of his actions were not only illegal but in direct violation of the most elementary principles of honour.

The results of Bentley's misgovernment were felt long after his death. He had for thirty years or more confined offices, fellowships, and scholarships to his nominees and partisans. In time, by seniority, these obtained the control of the College, and in their turn selected their successors largely on grounds of friendship and good fellowship, though, warned by Bentley's career, no injustice was publicly done. Under this government the College settled down for half a century after Bentley's death into a comfortable port-drinking society, well content to leave troublesome matters alone and far from strait-laced. Discipline, however, was restored, and the finances of the College, which had been seriously injured by Bentley's malversations, were put in order.

The last taint of Bentley's system of favouritism was removed in 1787. It would seem that in the seventeenth century the examination for fellowships was conducted publicly with the object of securing the best men. Bentley altered this, treating the award as a piece of patronage, and selecting candidates on the result of private interviews. After his death the Master and Senior Fellows, in whom the election was vested, continued the plan introduced by him of each elector examining candidates only informally and in private. Finally, some of them dispensed with any examination and merely attended the election. In 1786 a protest against this was made by some of the junior Fellows, and in consequence of an appeal to the Visitor, the matter came before the Lord Chancellor. Thurlow, in delivering judgment, condemned the practice that had grown up, but adjourned the appeal in the hope that further legal proceedings would be unnecessary.

The Seniors, to their credit, accepted the judgment, made subsequent elections impartially, and in no way hindered those

83

younger Fellows who now threw themselves into the task of restoring the traditions of the College. Of these perhaps the most remarkable was Thomas Jones, who about this time became a Tutor. No doubt the action of the reforming party was facilitated by the improvement which then became noticeable in the general standard of morality—an improvement of which the Simeon movement, referred to below, was partly the cause and partly the outcome.

One of the reforms they introduced, 1790, was a system of annual College examinations, which afford a reasonable periodical test of the progress of students. Another was the rule, 1810, that undergraduates should be required to pass an Entrance Examination before commencing residence.

This period is notable for the large number of eminent Judges educated in the College. I may instance J. S. Copley (Lord Lyndhurst), J. Williams, N. C. Tindal, J. Park (Lord Wensleydale), T. Coltman, F. Pollock, W. H. Maule, T. J. Platt, R. M. Cranworth (Lord Rolfe), J. Wigram, and E. H. Alderson. It is said that the strict training in geometry and formal logic then enforced on all candidates for high academical honours was favourable to the development of legal talent—it was a course designed to teach men how to think and learn rather than to give them definite information.

The usual subjects of study at this time

were mathematics, classics, and philosophy.
The Senate-House Examination, or Mathematical Tripos, afforded the chief avenue
of distinction to undergraduates. On the
social side of College life, say, from 1760
to 1820, I content myself by noting only
one or two details. University society
seems at this time to have been divided
into rigorously defined classes ; such as
heads of houses, professors, fellows, bachelors, noblemen and fellow-commoners, pensioners, &c. Though there were many
exceptions, there was in general but little
social intercourse between men of different
standing. Even among undergraduates,
fellow-commoners and sizars, noblemen
and scholars, reading men and non-reading
men, were sharply divided in pursuits as
well as tastes, while there were no clubs
and societies like those of the present time,
including men of all types. This was in
marked contrast to the society of a hun-
dred years previously as well as to that of
to-day.

The religious movement known as
Simeonism affected certain classes of undergraduates so profoundly, and its influence was so beneficial, that it must at least
be noticed in passing. The influence of
Simeon, wide though it was, would have
been greater if his adherents had mixed
more freely with others, but it may be
that this was not then as easy as it seems
to us. Among other undergraduates mor-

85

ality was perhaps at the lowest ebb—excessive drinking, if not drunkenness, was common in certain sets, and possibly grosser forms of vice were not unusual—but the last traces of these habits disappeared in the course of the nineteenth century.

Swimming, fives, racquets, tennis, billiards, cricket, riding, shooting, and occasional bull-baiting were favourite amusements among the wealthier students : a grace of 1750 specially mentions cricket - grounds and billiard - rooms as places where students wasted their time, and that even before noon ! Walking, bowls, quoits, and occasional outings on the river were usual relaxations of the more studious. The common habit of betting led to various feats of skill and strength—thus, in 1768, Rowland Hill, subsequently well known as a nonconformist divine, swam from Cambridge to Grantchester. Wine and tea parties were common, while breakfast parties (but not at very early hours) were given by those who studied economy. The only permanent clubs of which I have read were for dining, debating, music, and bell-ringing.

At this time prominent residents in College were Porson, who was elected to a fellowship in 1782, and subsequently held the Greek chair, and Mansel, Master from 1798 to 1820, and Bishop of Bristol from 1808. Both had a caustic wit, and many anecdotes relating to them are still extant. The former had unusual conversational powers, and an extraordinary power of composing at a moment's notice verses on any given subject. The lines known to every schoolboy,

> " When Dido found Æneas would not come
> She wept in silence and was Di-do-dum(b),"

were given offhand in answer to a challenge to compose a couplet involving the Latin gerunds. His remark, οὐτὲ τόδε οὐδὲ τάλλο, when he found himself one night with no whiskey at hand and in the dark, and his inscription, τῷ Βάκχῳ, scratched on one of the College silver tobacco jars, are well known. His criticisms, even when hostile, were not unkindly in form : " Mr. Southey," said he, on being asked his opinion of the poet, " is indeed a wonderful writer ; his works will be read when Homer and Virgil are forgotten." A characteristic story of him, which I have printed elsewhere, refers to his retort to a critic, J. T. Mathias (Fellow, 1776), who in an anonymous work had made some reflections on the critical abilities of Porson. Porson met Mathias in King's Parade, and remarked that rumour assigned to him the authorship of the criticism in question. " No," replied Mathias, " I did not write it ; I have nothing to do with it." " Oh," said Porson, " then I am glad of the opportunity to tell you that the writer of it is a confounded liar."

Mansel was an able man, but did not

enjoy the respect of his contemporaries, one of whom publicly described him as the "right reverend lover of small beer, the churchman's shame, the scholar's scorn, Lampoon and Epigram in lawn." Here is a story about him, more harmless than some. It is said that one of the undergraduates invariably walked across the grass on his way to Hall. One day the Master determined to reprove the delinquent, and, opening the window at which he was sitting, he called to the student, "Sir, I never look out of my window but I see you walking across the grass plot." "My lord," replied the offender, "I never walk across the grass plot but I see you looking out of your window." It is, however, a familiar fact that numbers of anecdotes are standing stories, assigned by each generation to some one in the near past who has a reputation for wit, but as I know of no earlier mention of this story, it may be that Mansel was the first to whom the retort was made.

CHAPTER VI

THE NINETEENTH CENTURY RENAISSANCE

MANSEL died in 1820, and was succeeded in the mastership by Christopher Wordsworth, the brother of the poet.
Wordsworth was not a strong man, nor
always judicious, but he had the good of the
Society at heart, and was ever willing to
spend himself in its service. The building
of the New Court was undertaken on his
initiative. The time of his accession was
one of considerable intellectual activity, and
opens a new era in the history of the
College.

At this time, conspicuous among the
Fellows of Trinity were A. Sedgwick, the
geologist; G. Peacock, the mathematician;
J. Scholfield, Julius C. Hare, and C. Thirlwall, the well-known scholars; and G. B.
Airy, the astronomer. It would be difficult
to exaggerate their influence on the intellectual life of the College and University.
The undergraduate society a few years
later numbered a group of men of exceptional power, notably R. C. Trench, afterwards Archbishop of Dublin, W. M.
Thackeray, Edward Fitzgerald, Monckton
Milnes (Lord Houghton), James Spedding,

the biographer of Bacon, A. H. Hallam,
A. W. Kinglake, the historian, Alfred,
Charles, and Frederick Tennyson, and
W. H. Thompson. T. B. Macaulay,
Fellow 1824, was of somewhat earlier date;

AVENUE AND NEW COURT

while Henry Alford and E. L. Lushington,
Fellows 1834, and J. Grote, Fellow 1837,
all well-known Greek scholars, are of a
somewhat later date. Their memoirs and
letters give us a full picture of their student
life. Doubtless the above form a striking

90

cluster of names, but it would be difficult to pick out a single decade subsequent to 1787 in which two-thirds of the Fellows elected were not men who subsequently became eminent in the literary, scientific, or political world.

In 1834 the Master took the high-handed course of removing Thirlwall, afterwards Bishop of St. Davids, from the office of Assistant-Tutor, on the ground that he had expressed the opinion that it would be better if attendance at Chapel were made voluntary and not enforced as an act of discipline. It is said that Wordsworth argued that the only alternatives between which they had to choose were compulsory religion and no religion, to which Thirlwall replied that he regretted he had to confess that the distinction between them was too subtle for his mental grasp. Wordsworth's action was condemned by many of the residents, and perhaps was unstatutable, but Thirlwall refused to appeal to the Visitor in defence of his rights.

In 1840 Wordsworth resigned the mastership, at the same time urging on the Prime Minister the qualifications of Whewell for the post. To Whewell it was offered, and the result more than justified Wordsworth's opinion.

Whewell's abilities and strong personality had made him the most prominent resident at this time, and for some years Wordsworth had acted largely on Whewell's advice.

The latter had then just vacated the tutorship. In this office he had not been successful : he had not made its duties his main work, his attention was absorbed in other pursuits, while to his pupils he was neither sympathetic nor readily accessible—a truly damning indictment. But the mastership offered him opportunities for leadership, encouragement of learning, and unselfish munificence of which he freely availed himself.

The first serious task to which Whewell set himself was the revision of the College statutes, with the object not so much of introducing changes as of bringing them into accord with existing practice. The result was the code of 1844.

Whewell was more interested in the promotion of learning than his immediate predecessors. Subjects, other than the time-honoured classics and mathematics — such as science, philosophy, and history— were warmly encouraged by him in the College as also in the University, and in the organisation of studies he suggested many improvements. The great development of the science schools, which may be dated from this time, was largely due to him. The plan of allowing residence during a considerable part of the Long Vacation was also introduced on his suggestion.

A considerable party in the College, however, now became prominent, who desired changes of a more revolutionary character. They argued that the University

and Colleges did not make the best use of
their position and property, and that the
Elizabethan statutes were out of date.
Finally, a Royal Commission was appointed to report on the matter. As a
consequence new statutes were made for
the University and all the Colleges therein.
Without going into details it may be said
that the resulting College statutes of 1860
curtailed the power of the Master, reducing
him to the position of the president of an
executive council, though possessed of considerable powers of initiative and control :
the whole body of Fellows were to
meet at least once a year, and on certain
questions their decision was to be final ;
Fellows on the College staff were not
required to take Orders, but in the case
of other Fellows the obligation to do so
remained as a condition of tenure after
seven years from M.A. standing : celibacy,
however, continued enforced except in the
case of professors and a few specified officers.
To most of these changes Whewell gave
only a reluctant consent.

In 1857 advantage was taken of the
proposed revision of the statutes to procure
the consent of the authorities of Westminster School to the abolition of the
rights enjoyed by three of their scholars
to succeed, if properly qualified, each year
to scholarships in the College. In lieu of
this the College agreed to found for Westminster boys three close exhibitions which

93

should be tenable in addition to College
emoluments gained in open competition.
The need for additional chambers was

TURRET IN WHEWELL'S COURT

urgent, and Whewell at his own cost erected,
bartly in 1859, partly in 1866, the Courts
associated with his name: they were finished
by his executors. The total cost is said to

94

have exceeded £100,000. The buildings were given to the College, but the rents received are held on trust for various objects.

In 1863 Whewell was responsible for a dispute as to whether the lodging of the Judges in College was an obligation or a matter of courtesy. From the opinions given by Fitzroy Kelly, Hugh Cairns, and FitzJames Stephens it seems, first, that the Lodge is not in any way a royal residence, and, second, that the reception of the Judges originated in an invitation voluntarily given and was not a matter of right on their part. On the other hand, I conceive that the Crown could on a vacancy in the mastership obtain the right to use the Lodge or a part of it by altering the form of the letters patent granting the office. The College, however, regarded it as a privilege to entertain the Judges when on Assize, and in deference to the very strong opinion expressed on the subject Whewell, albeit with rather scanty grace, consented to allow the practice to continue.

Whewell died in 1866. It is said that science was his forte, but omniscience his foible. His intellectual powers and knowledge were immense, though he was so conscious of the fact as to render it an easy matter for jokes, as witness Sir Francis Doyle—

"If you through the regions of space should have
    travelled,
And of nebular films the remotest unravelled,
You'll find as you tread on the bounds of infinity,
That God's greatest work is the Master of Trinity."

He was unfitted for tutorial work, and it is said was even unacquainted with many of his pupils. There is a College anecdote to the effect that when he and two of his colleagues, whom I will term A and B, were examining for scholarships, general distrust was felt of A because he was so afraid of being biassed that he always voted against his own pupils; equal distrust was felt of B, who never voted for any but his own pupils; but universal confidence was felt in Whewell, since he never knew who were his pupils and who were not.

Stories of his rudeness, especially to undergraduates, are common. To one, who had offered acceptable shelter in a thunderstorm, he is said to have forbidden conversation by reminding his benefactor that by the College rules no communication was permissible between the Master and an undergraduate except through the latter's Tutor. To another, whom he saw smoking in the Great Court, he propounded the fearful dilemma: "Do you mean, sir, to deliberately insult me, or are you totally lost to a sense of decency?" The man made the best reply, saying, "If you please, Sir, I am totally lost to a sense of decency." In truth, Whewell was absurdly punctilious on trifles, if he thought they in any way affected his dignity as Master, of which he was ever conscious. And even to his equals he was often gruff and rude. But these are only the spots on the sun. Of his generosity, magnanimity, and conscientiousness it is difficult to speak too highly ; and of his affection for the College there was no doubt. He used to say that the sky never looked so blue as when framed by the battlements of the Great Court, and, when dying, almost his last wish was to be lifted up so as to see, through the windows, its ancient walls and turrets under the light of the morning sun.

Whewell was succeeded by Thompson, one of the finest Greek scholars of his generation. In his lectures it may be said that he carried on the traditions of Porson, Julius Hare, and Thirlwall ; he had fine critical judgment, and he had made a careful study of Greek philosophy.

Immediately on Thompson's accession, the College and the Home Secretary entered into negotiations with the object of preventing any friction arising in the future over the reception of the Judges. With the approval of the Lord Chief Justice and the law officers of the Crown, an instrument was executed giving, while it remained in force, the Judges of Assize a right to lodge in the College, and defining the hospitality to be offered to them.

The biological and medical schools received a considerable stimulus from the appointment by the College, in 1870, of a praelector in physiology. This, however, was only one aspect of an activity in the College which affected all studies. Under

Clerk Maxwell, Lord Rayleigh, and J. J. Thomson, the school of mathematical and experimental physics was greatly developed; while the names of Munro and Jebb in classics; of Jackson in Greek philosophy; of Sidgwick in ethics; and of Westcott, Lightfoot, and Hort, in theology, will occur to all as among eminent residents of the period. All of these were Fellows of the College.

Two internal reforms of considerable importance were introduced at this time. The first was a recognition of the principle that all educational appointments and payments were made directly by the College, and not by the Master or Tutors. The second was the introduction into the fellowship examination of a system of dissertations, which has served to encourage original work by young graduates.

The most important event in Thompson's mastership was a fresh revision of the College statutes. In 1872 the College drafted a new code, which led to the appointment of Commissions to collect information and draft statutes for the University and all the Colleges therein. By the College statutes, as finally approved in 1882, the government of the College was vested in an executive council of thirteen members; the whole body of Fellows was given a decisive voice on fundamental questions; all restrictions on marriage were discarded; a time limit to the tenure of offices was established;

a system of pensions on retirement from office was introduced; and arrangements made by which fellowships could be given for research work.

Thompson died in 1886, and his death severed almost the last of the links which connected the College under the Elizabethan statutes with the College of to-day. His dignified presence, courtly manners, sound judgment, and shrewd criticism are still affectionately remembered. He was a brilliant conversationalist. His wit could be biting, but, in spite of the stories to the contrary, it was not used ungenerously. Every one quotes his remark, "We are none of us infallible, not even the youngest of us," made at a College meeting when one of the junior Fellows brought forward some sweeping proposals which should introduce the millennium. Of an ill-informed philanthropist who had tried to cover a bad blunder by deprecating intellectual pride, he remarked, "He talks about pride of intellect; it is a temptation he never experienced." His comment on a man who did not carry out the duties of an office which he held, "He devotes to the neglect of his duties the time that he spares from the adornment of his person," is severe, but it would be necessary to know the facts before condemning it. To a lady who gushed over the elaborated writings of a certain divine, and justified her opinion to Thompson by saying, "You know, Master, he has so much taste," he made the not unfitting reply, " Yes, and all so bad." But stories such as these, without their setting, give a false impression of the man. His manner was severe, but his coldness was only on the surface. It is said he never lost a friend, and of his courtesy and warm-heartedness no one who knew him could doubt.

Dr. Butler, the present Head of the College, succeeded to the mastership on Thompson's death.

During the Victorian Renaissance the constitution of the College and life at it underwent sweeping changes. In the early half of the nineteenth century the schemes of education and examination were simple. To-day there are endless subjects of study, and the intellectual life of the place is too complex to be described in a few sentences. In social matters also the organisation of amusements and of clubs (literary, scientific, athletic, &c.) has developed to a marvellous extent. On the whole, however, we may say that the ordinary undergraduate works harder, and leads a simpler life, though in more luxurious surroundings, than his predecessors.

Here I conclude my brief account of the College. As a last word it may be well to add that I have confined myself to its external aspects and history. Of the spirit that actuates it, of all that makes it a living Society, I have said nothing. In truth, these are incapable of analysis. The charm that the place perennially exercises on those who, generation after generation, make it their home, the affection it inspires, are intangible. They exist, and there are but few members of the House who have not felt them, but they can be appreciated only by those who have shared in its life and dwelt within its walls.

INDEX

INDEX

INDEX

INDEX

INDEX

THE END

For EU product safety concerns, contact us at Calle de José Abascal, 56–1°, 28003 Madrid, Spain or eugpsr@cambridge.org.

 www.ingramcontent.com/pod-product-compliance
Ingram Content Group UK Ltd.
Pitfield, Milton Keynes, MK11 3LW, UK
UKHW012338130625
459647UK00009B/363